LIFE IN A
VIKING TOWN

JANE SHUTER

Heinemann
LIBRARY

www.heinemann.co.uk/library
Visit our website to find out more information about
Heinemann Library books.

To order:
☎ Phone 44 (0) 1865 888066
🖹 Send a fax to 44 (0) 1865 314091
💻 Visit the Heinemann Bookshop at
www.heinemann.co.uk/library to browse our catalogue and
order online.

First published in Great Britain by
Heinemann Library, Halley Court, Jordan
Hill, Oxford OX2 8EJ, part of Harcourt
Education.
Heinemann is a registered trademark of
Harcourt Education Ltd.

© Harcourt Education Ltd 2005

Editors: Nancy Dickmann and
    Sarah Chappelow
Design: Ron Kamen and
    Dave Oakley/Arnos Design
Illustrations: Barry Atkinson
Maps: Jeff Edwards
Picture Researcher: Erica Newbery
    and Elaine Willis
Production Controller: Camilla Smith

Originated by Modern Age
Printed in China by WKT Company Limited

ISBN 0 431 04297 7
09 08 07 06 05
10 9 8 7 6 5 4 3 2 1

British Library Cataloguing in Publication
Data
Shuter, Jane
Life in a Viking town. - (Picture the past)
948'.022
A full catalogue record for this book is
available from the British Library.

Acknowledgements:
The publishers would like to thank the
following for permission to reproduce
photographs: AAAC p. **16**; AKG pp. **14**, **20**
(Schijtze/Rodemann); Bergin Field and
James p. **8**; Bridgeman p. **28**; British
Museum p. **24**; Corbis pp. **6** (Richard T.
Nowitz), **12** (Archivo Iconografico);
National Museum of Denmark p. **11**;
Werner Forman pp. **10**, **22**, **29** (National
Museum of Iceland, Reykjavik); York
Archaeological Trust pp. **13**, **18**, **23**.

Cover photograph of a wood carving
showing a Viking blacksmith at work,
reproduced with permission of Picture
Desk.

Every effort has been made to contact
copyright holders of any material
reproduced in this book. Any omissions will
be rectified in subsequent printings if
notice is given to the publishers.

Contents

Any words appearing in bold, **like this**, are explained in the Glossary.

Who were the Vikings?

The Vikings lived in Norway, Sweden and Denmark, more than 1,000 years ago. They had a reputation for being **raiders** who attacked without warning. There were many different groups of Vikings, each with their own leader. At first, the Vikings lived in small **settlements**. Then they began to live, work and **trade** in towns. The Vikings who lived in towns had different lives from those who lived in the countryside.

Look for these: The chessmen show you the subject of each chapter. The picture stone shows you boxes with interesting facts, figures, and quotes about life in a Viking town.

TIMELINE OF EVENTS IN THIS BOOK

AD 700 Vikings spread across Norway, Denmark, and Sweden

AD 780 First Viking raids on England

AD 795 First Viking raids on Ireland

AD 799 First Viking raids on France

VIKINGS MOVE ACROSS EUROPE, SAILING UP MAJOR RIVERS AD 800–850

AD 800 Birka (Sweden), Hedeby (Denmark), Kaupang (Norway) start to grow as trading towns

AD 836 Vikings set up Dublin which becomes a trading town in the 880s

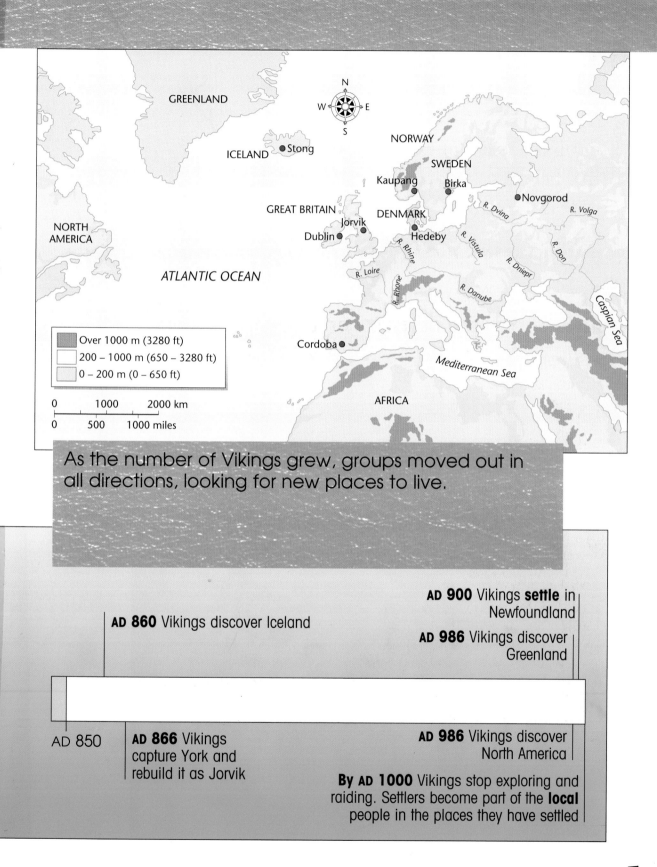

As the number of Vikings grew, groups moved out in all directions, looking for new places to live.

AD 900 Vikings **settle** in Newfoundland

AD 860 Vikings discover Iceland

AD 986 Vikings discover Greenland

AD 850

AD 866 Vikings capture York and rebuild it as Jorvik

AD 986 Vikings discover North America

By AD 1000 Vikings stop exploring and raiding. Settlers become part of the **local** people in the places they have settled

Viking towns

The earliest Vikings lived in small farming **settlements**. However, as they began to **trade**, some settlements grew into trading places. More and more people came to these trading places, and they grew into towns. Often, these towns had walls and gates to keep out **raiders** from other Viking groups.

Once Vikings began to live in towns, there were more strangers around. They began to lock away their valuables with keys like these ones.

BIGGER KINGDOMS

From the year AD 700 onwards, the strongest leaders began to unite Viking groups into bigger and bigger **kingdoms**. The bigger a kingdom, the more warriors it had, so the more powerful it was. The king ruled from a large town with a wall around it.

The Vikings did not call in the builders when they wanted a new home! They and their neighbours built the house together, to the same pattern. Homes in towns were often **workshops** too.

Viking craft workers had workshops in their homes. You can see a blacksmith and a wood worker in the yards of their homes.

Who lived where?

The street names in **Jorvik** tell us that different craft workers lived in different parts of the town. Viking craft workers **specialized** in making just one thing. They made shoes, cups, or knives and sold them to other people from their **workshops**. All the shoemakers lived in one area, all the cup makers in another area, and so on.

NAMES

Some Viking names look like modern words, but they don't always mean the same. The Viking for "cup makers" was "kopari" and "street" was "gata". So Coppergate was the cup makers' street. It was not where the copper makers worked.

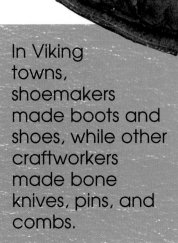

In Viking towns, shoemakers made boots and shoes, while other craftworkers made bone knives, pins, and combs.

This is a modern artist's view of the Viking town of Jorvik from the air, drawn from evidence found by **archaeologists**.

Docks and trade

Trade was important to the Vikings, and it helped their towns to develop quickly. The Vikings traded some things **locally**, in their own towns. These were everyday things such as shoes, pottery, wooden chests, and tools and weapons. Craftworkers sold them to people in the town or from the nearby **settlements**.

SLAVES

When they attacked other places, the Vikings often captured women and children, and sometimes men too. They then kept these people as **slaves**, or sold them when they next went trading.

The Vikings sometimes used silver to pay for things, and charged by the weight of the silver. Viking traders took their own scales and weights, like these, to check other traders' weighing.

The Vikings also traded with people from far away. They traded **goods** they had plenty of, such as furs, honey, and fish, for goods such as silk and spices. They traded at least as far west as Greenland, as far east as Russia, and as far south as the North African coast. The goods they bought sometimes came from even further away. Goods from as far away as India have been found in Viking graves.

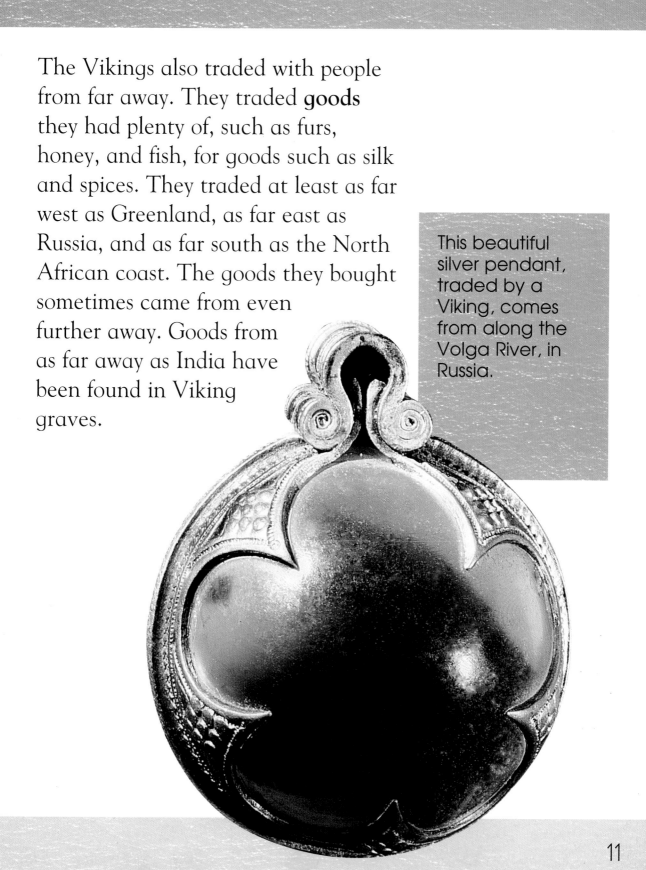

This beautiful silver pendant, traded by a Viking, comes from along the Volga River, in Russia.

Work

Most people in towns were **specialized** craftworkers, making things such as pots. People came from all around to buy their goods. These craftworkers had **workshops** in the front of their home, on the street. They sold from their workshops or a stall. People who had no skills tried to make a living by fetching and carrying for the workshop owners, or working as servants in the homes of the rich.

The craftworker who made this **brooch** probably charged a lot for it. But he had to pay a lot for the gold he made it with. He also had to spend a lot of time learning how to work with gold.

The Viking towns of Hedeby, in Denmark, and **Jorvik**, have both been **excavated**. **Archaeologists** found **evidence** of craftworkers making objects from metal and bone in both these towns. They also found evidence that jewellers, glassmakers, potters, woodworkers, and ropemakers had worked there. There were also many leatherworkers, who made boots, shoes, purses, and belts.

LEARNING A CRAFT

Viking craftworkers learned their **trade** by working for a skilled craftworker from about the age of ten. Workshops often had three or four workers at different stages of learning their craft.

Bone objects, like these, were quickly made from cheap materials, but they had to be sold cheaply, too.

Warriors

Viking men did not just have one job – they all had to be **warriors** and **raiders** too. The king of each Viking group had to be able to lead all the men in battle. Viking men went exploring and raiding all the time in the summer, leaving the women to run things at home. They always took their weapons, expecting to have to fight somewhere along the way.

Well-made Viking swords were often handed down from father to son. Some were even given names like "foe biter", which means "destroy the enemy".

The people of the town took it in turns to guard the walls and search the **local** countryside if they thought they might be attacked.

WEAPONS

The Vikings fought with swords, spears, and axes. They had metal helmets and wooden shields edged with metal or leather to protect them. Shields had to reach from shoulder to knee and were usually round.

Homes

Houses in Viking towns were built on pieces of land with fences around them. What they were made from and how they were made, depended on where the town was. In cold places, the Vikings dug out the floor to below ground level, which made homes warmer. In Greenland, homes were made from stone covered with earth and grass. In Britain and Europe, homes were made from wood and thatch.

OUTSIDE THE HOUSE

Viking homes in towns usually had pens for chickens and animals as well as a toilet outside the house. They often had a garden to grow fruit and vegetables in too.

Buckets were important in a Viking home. All the water for washing and cooking had to be fetched from a nearby well.

Viking women made cloth for the family clothes on looms.

The cooking **hearth** had stones around the edge for safety. It was the only heating.

Wide benches down either side, made of wood or earth, were used for sleeping or sitting.

The floors were made of earth.

Homes had small windows or none at all, so they were dark and airless.

Family life

Families were very important to the Vikings. In early Viking times, everyone in a **settlement** was often related. They lived in large family groups and took pride in knowing their family's history. The men of different families arranged marriages between their children, but a Viking girl could reject a possible husband. Divorce was not hard if a couple were unhappy.

WOMEN

Viking women did not go to war with men. They were not **raiders**. They did not trade either. But they could own their own property and run the family farm or business while their husbands were away.

Women rubbed stones, like these, against cloth to help make it smooth.

Children in towns did not begin to learn a **trade** until about the age of ten. Children born in a farming settlement would start helping with the work on the farm from a very young age.

Boys who lived in towns often helped their fathers when they were very small, before going away to learn a trade.

Education

Children were brought up in the family home until they were about ten. After that, boys were often sent to live with other families. There they would learn a **trade** and how to fight. The sons of important Vikings did not need to learn a trade, but they may have learned to read, or understand the law. The children usually went to live with relatives or friends of the family.

A LEADER'S SKILLS

One leader lists the other things he had to learn: "I can write well, I can read, and mend a sword easily. I can ski, fire arrows, and row well. I can recite poetry and play music." A **saga** said a leader also had to be a brave **warrior**.

Writing was important to the Vikings. They used knives to carve letters (runes) on to stone or wood.

Viking girls learned to run a home, while boys learned a skill. Childhood did not last long. A boy was treated as an adult from about the age of twelve and some girls were married at that age.

This boy is learning to be a blacksmith. Before he learned to beat metal into shape he had to learn to get the fire to just the right heat by blowing air into it with a leather bag called a bellows.

Free time

In most parts of the Viking world, the long dark winters cut short the working day. So, the Vikings had a lot of free time. The Vikings played different board games. They loved poetry and storytelling. Often, the women wove cloth and the men carved wood while listening to a story. They liked clever tricks with language too, like riddles and proverbs.

RIDDLES

A good riddle was a rhyming description of an ordinary object. They could be very long and difficult. This riddle is short:
On the way a miracle: water becomes bone (answer on page 30).

This is a game where one side has a king and his warriors. The other side has no king but more warriors. They have to try to capture the king.

For much of the Viking period, stories were not written down, so people had to learn them by heart. At feasts, storytellers called skalds told stories. Most skalds were men. They were especially good at telling stories. They remembered stories that could go on for hours. The stories usually rhymed, to make them easier to remember. Skalds also had to be able to make up stories about events in their group, such a victory in battle.

The Vikings made their own music. Their musical instruments were made of wood and bone. Many people made their own.

Clothes

Most Vikings wore the same kinds of clothes, usually made from wool. The women of the family spun, dyed, and wove the cloth themselves. They used vegetable dyes. These could be quite bright to begin with, but soon faded. Rich Vikings could buy expensive fabrics, like silk, from **traders** in towns.

SILK

Only kings and rich people could afford clothes made from silk. They bought the silk at the market and slaves made the clothes for them. Because the silk came all the way from China, it was very expensive.

The Vikings had simple hairstyles. They carried combs with them, to keep their hair (and the men's beards) tidy.

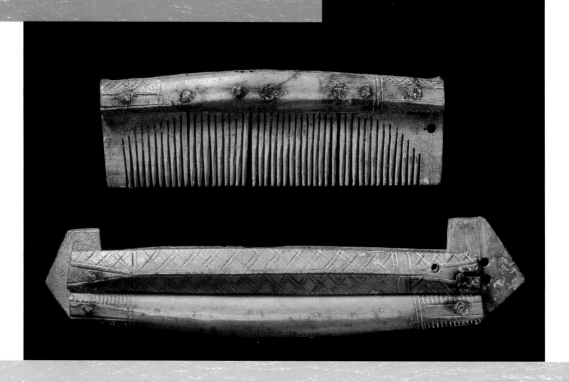

Women and girls wore long dresses covered with an apron when they were working. Men and boys wore trousers and a **tunic**. Cloaks tied with a **brooch** were the usual sort of covering for going outdoors. Shoes, boots, and belts were made from leather.

Vikings dressed to fit the weather. In cold places they lined their boots with fur. They also changed the way they dressed to fit in with **local** people. Traders did this, and so did **settlers** who moved to live in newly discovered lands.

Food and drink

The Vikings ate two meals a day, in the morning and in the evening. They cooked over an open fire on a **hearth** in the middle of their houses, using iron pots and pans. They ate a lot of meat and fish, bread, cheese, and vegetables. They grew and raised most of the food they ate themselves.

Some iron pots stood on legs over the fire. Others were hung from the roof on a chain that hooked over the handle of the pot. You can see the holes for handles on these pots.

Berry pudding

The Vikings would have cooked this dish over an open fire, but you can do it in an oven instead.

WARNING: do not cook anything unless there is an adult to help you.

You will need:
155g (5.5 oz) white flour
155g (5.5 oz) wholemeal flour
1/2 teaspoon of salt
450ml (3/4 pint) of milk
25g (1oz) of butter
1 cup of berries

1 Pre-heat the oven to 225°C (425°F).

2 Mix the salt and the two flours together.

3 Slowly add the milk, stirring, then whisking, with a fork as you go.

4 Melt the butter in a shallow baking tray in the oven.

5 Stir the berries into the batter and pour the batter into the pan.

6 Cook for about 20 minutes (take out when it is golden brown).

Religion

The early Vikings believed in many different gods and goddesses. They thought that these gods and goddesses controlled everyday life. They had to be kept happy with prayers and presents. The Vikings imagined the gods as living all together in heaven in a big family group, arguing, fighting, and making up, just like Viking families.

MAIN GODS

Thor	god of storms
Odin	god of war
Frey	god of growing things
Freya	Frey's sister

This hammer-shaped charm is the symbol of the god Thor, the god of thunder (because thunder makes a hammering sound). It has a Christian cross on it too, because some Vikings were Christians.

Some Vikings became Christian. Sometimes this was because some Christians would only trade with other Christians. Sometimes a Christian king who defeated a Viking in battle would make him change religion. Many Christian Vikings still worshipped their old gods, even though Christianity said not to do this.

Vikings who became Christian built churches like this one to worship in. The Vikings probably went to special places outdoors to worship their other gods, such as Thor.

Glossary

archaeologist person who finds objects from long ago to work out how people lived in the past

brooch piece of jewellery to pin on to clothing

evidence something that tells you what happened

excavate when things are dug out of the ground, layer by layer. This is usually done by an archaeologist, who keeps a note of what she or he has found.

goods things that are bought and sold

hearth fireproof, safe, place indoors to build a fire for cooking and/or heating

Jorvik Viking city in the north of England, now the city of York

kingdom all the land and people that are controlled by one leader

local nearby

raiders people who go to a place to take things from the people who live there by force

saga Viking adventure story

settle move from one place to live in another

settlement place where people live and bring up their families for many years

slaves person who is bought and sold by someone and has to work for them

specialized to do just one job, not lots of jobs

trade this can mean:

1 a job

2 selling or swapping goods

tunic clothing shaped like a T-shirt that came to about the knees

warrior person trained to fight in battle

workshop place where several people work together to make something

Answer to the riddle on page 22:

an icicle

Further resources

Books
Explore History: Romans, Anglo-Saxons & Vikings in Britain (Heinemann Library, 2001)
The Saxons and the Vikings (Heinemann Library, 1994)
The Viking World, Christine Hatt (Heinemann Library, 2004)
What happened here?: Viking Street, Marilyn Tolhurst (A & C Black ,1994)

Websites
www.jorvik-viking-centre.co.uk/jorvik-navigation.htm
Use this website to find out all about the Vikings and visit the Jorvik Viking Centre online.

www.pbs.org/wgbh/nova/vikings/
An exciting website that contains video clips to bring the Vikings to life!

www.bbc.co.uk/history/ancient/vikings/
A website packed with information, activities, and animations about the Vikings

www.mnh.si.edu/vikings/start.html
Go on a Viking voyage and learn all about their sagas on this website.

Contacts
Jorvik Viking Centre
Coppergate, York, YO1 9WT

Email: jorvik@yorkarchaeology.co.uk
Tel: 01904 643211

Disclaimer
All the Internet addresses (URLs) given in this book were valid at the time of going to press. However, due to the dynamic nature of the Internet, some addresses may have changed, or sites may have ceased to exist since publication. While the author and publishers regret any inconvenience this may cause readers, no responsibility for any such changes can be accepted by either the author or the publishers.

Index

Titles in the *Picture the Past* series include:

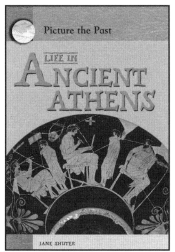

Hardback 0431042942

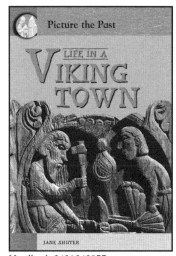

Hardback 0431042977

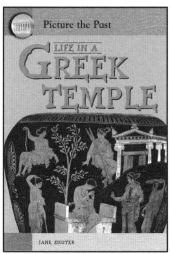

Hardback 0431042950

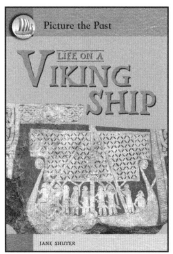

Hardback 0431042985

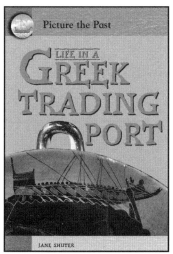

Hardback 0431042969

Find out about the other titles in this series on our website www.heinemann.co.uk/library